The Lives We Live

Understanding that intersections and detours are designed to fulfill God's plan for our lives

Edited by Critique Editing Services
www.critiqueyourbook.com

Author: Sepsimone Johnson

The Lives We Live

Copyright © 2014 Sepsimone Johnson
sepsimonejohnson.webs.com

No part of this book can be reproduced without written permission from the author.

All characters are fictional and any similarities to real characters, living or dead, places, or events are merely products of the author's imagination. Any resemblance is entirely coincidental.

Cover Design by:

Langao
From: www.fiverr.com/langao

ISBN-13: 978-1499165647

Dedication

I would like to thank my husband for being a supportive and smart man. Anytime I ask him a question he always has an answer. To my daughter whom I pray over daily, that she will continue to allow the Holy Spirit to lead her. To my mom and dad who know that I'm different, and love to try new things, and applaud me through them all because I'm the baby girl. And my sister who has jumped on my entire band wagon of ideas, and stayed on for the ride.

During prayer time in my closet one morning: "Lord, use me today for Your glory. Use me as a vessel," is what I asked Him. I never would have imagined that it would have turned into a book. I sat down and wrote, and wrote some more. My thoughts were going so fast that my pen could not keep up. Not really sure if I came up for food or water. I did not stop that day until it was complete.

And here you have it, *The Lives We Live*. A compilation of short stories that I pray will inspire, motivate and encourage, you to step from behind the curtain, pull the covers away from your head, and be all that God has called you to be.

Anna

Anna, was a single mom, whose idea of showing her children love was to buy them the latest fashions, gadgets and toys, which for her meant working more hours, and spending less time at home with them.

The night shift had begun and Anna received a phone call; one that she would have rather not received. Her daughter, Sunshine told her that Esquire, her son was playing with matches and caught the house on fire. Anna began to panic and wondered what to do. She asked if everyone was ok; Sunshine told her yes, and that the firemen were on the way. Anna darted home. When she arrived on the scene the firemen had already begun to put the fire out. She was devastated. All she could do was drop to her knees and weep. Anna was in total shock. Once she regained her composure, she questioned her children. They were trying to explain and at the same time play the blame game.

Because Anna was new to the area, she had no one to turn to. Her family lived out of state. The officers that were dispatched gave her directions to a shelter. Anna looked at her home in disbelief. You name it, everything was charred; nothing was salvageable. Anna remembered in the past Stacy, her co-worker speaking to her about her church and how they would help people in need. Anna wasn't sure they would work with her, seeing as though she hadn't gone to church in over 10 years. The shelter provided 3 meals a day and also clothing. The children continued to go to school as Anna continued to go to work.

After being in the shelter a week she was over it; Anna knew that she needed to do something different. Stacy once again mentioned that her church would help out. She had been a little hesitant about mentioning it to Anna because she knew how prideful she was. Anna asked what the catch was; she wanted to know what her obligations would be. In the meantime, Anna was trying to hold things together, but she could no longer do it.

The next day at work she asked Stacy what the next steps would be. Stacy picked up the phone and called her church. They told her that Anna could come by immediately. Once Anna arrived they had food, clothing and keys to a house for her. Anna was overjoyed. She could not believe that these people, who had no idea who she was, could be so kind. She thanked her co-worker and the church.

This gave Anna a different outlook on church. Unfortunately, Anna had had bad experiences with the church that she'd kept inside for years. Anna and her children began to become more involved in the church that assisted them in their time of need. Her heart softened toward God and his people. She joined the single mothers' ministry, which taught her that one of the most important things that children need is their parents. Not things, but attention, love, and affection from her. She opened up to the other single mothers more and more as they met. She learned so much about being a mom. Even though Anna and her children lost everything, they still had each other. God will remove everything from us, if need be, to get our attention. Answer Him today while he's calling your name.

Alan

Alan could not believe he was walking across the stage to receive his Doctorate in Medicine. Alan wanted to specialize in pediatric internal medicine. He wasn't sure whether he should start with the hospital where he did his residency or open his own clinic. People advised him to start with the local hospital, get his feet wet, and then he could venture out on his own.

Alan was a high achiever; he was always the first to volunteer. He knew what he wanted and he went after it.

Alan decided to start out at the hospital; he had 4 days on, and 3 days off. He didn't mind it at first. One month, two months, and three months went by and he started to become more sensitive to the children he started to see. He asked his colleagues how they coped with seeing so many sick and helpless children; they told him that over time he would become immune to it.

Alan began to feel so overwhelmed with work that he started to second guess if this was what God called him to do. That night, unlike others, was dragging by pretty slowly. He went into the doctor's quarters to try and catch up on some shut-eye. He felt like he had drifted off, but not really. Alan heard someone say, "What are you doing here?" He jumped up and looked around and saw no one; at that time he received a page from the ER. Alan headed down the hall, when he was approached by Phillip and Stephanie, the parents of Carson, who had just been admitted. Carson had a rare blood disease that his meds were no longer able to treat. He assured them that he would do all he could to help their son. Alan started to do research while spending countless hours at the hospital. He would occasionally recall the voice that he heard asking him what he was doing there, but thought nothing further about it.

Phillip and Stephanie were missionaries and happened to be back in the States visiting family, when Carson had an episode. Phillip saw how hard Alan was working to come up with a cure for their son, and asked him if he had ever thought about going out of the country to practice medicine. Alan was in total shock because right at that moment the Holy Spirit brought back to his remembrance what was whispered to him in the residency room. Phillip began to tell Alan how they assisted those who were less fortunate in other countries. Alan could not believe what he was hearing. That thought was really tugging on his heart. At that moment he realized what his calling was.

Alan was always told as a child that he would make a difference in the world one day, but being a child, he wasn't sure what that meant.

The couple saw something in Alan that they felt was Christ like; they knew he had a heart for people, especially children.

Alan completed his time in the States and was able to join Phillip and Stephanie overseas. Carson had been cured of the disease because of Alan's determination. Alan was somewhat of a carnal Christian, but when he realized his calling, and surrendered, nothing could stop him from doing what God called him to do.

Reid

Reid grew up in a home where he felt confined; he could not hang out with a particular group of friends, go to the school dances, listen to certain kinds of music, watch certain television shows, or talk on the phone to certain friends. I forgot to mention that Reid was a PK (Preacher's Kid). You name it, Reid did it in the church from singing in the choir, to being an usher. He felt as though he was expected to do everything. By the time his senior year approached he was disgusted; he could not wait to leave after graduation.

Reid went away to college and was introduced to so many different religions. The one that he found interesting he said made him feel like he had no boundaries, which was something he wasn't used to. In that religion you did not have any accountability, and if you did something wrong it was ok, because you were still considered to be a good person, as long as you turned around and did something generous for someone. Reid began to avoid his parents,

Joseph and Susan's phone calls because he knew that if they found out, they would be furious. Reid became more and more involved with his new friends and religion, but something still seemed to be missing. He felt as though he had a void.

While back home Joseph and Susan continued to keep him lifted up in prayer, because by that time his mom started to have dreams that he was going astray. So she was determined to keep him covered; she knew that nothing was too hard for God. His parents had laid his foundation, but in the back of his mother's mind, while she felt that he was still her baby, she also knew he had to find his own way. So his mom continued to keep him covered, and in her prayer time she asked the Lord to send laborers across his path, that would help guide him back in the right direction. She also knew that she could pray God's word and it would not return to him void.

Days and weeks went by and Reid began to notice flyers at the school that bible studies were being held around campus, but he tried to ignore them. Students in class would get into debates over religion (Christianity in particular). They would turn and ask him what he thought, but he would simply say 'No comment.' They had no idea that he was a PK. Reid continued to see the flyers and posters around campus, so he finally decided to visit one of the bible study groups. He sat in the back of the room with his hat pulled down over his eyes. No one could see the tears that began to run down his cheeks and land on his shirt, as Russell, one of the student ministers stepped up to the podium to speak on the prodigal son. Reid could not believe what he was hearing and how God was so on time with the message.

Weeks later Reid saw Russell in the hallway; Reid looked the other way and began to pick up his pace. Russell said, "Excuse me, were you in bible study a few weeks ago?" Reid began to stutter and said, "Uh yea, uh that was me." He asked him if he enjoyed it. Reid told him he thought it was ok. At that time he asked Reid if he was a Christian. Reid paused for a minute and said, "Uh yea, well, uh yea," Russell said, "What does that mean?" Reid began to tell him that as a child he had accepted Jesus into his life, and that he grew up in the church but had gone astray. Russell told him, "You know that once you're saved, you're always saved, right?" Reid said, "Yes, but I've joined another religion. He said, "You've only broken the fellowship, but not the relationship with your heavenly Father." He invited Reid to the next bible study.

Reid showed up and sat closer to the front this time. Russell's message that day was about returning to your first love. And oh how the message touched his heart. Russell said, "There is nothing you can do that is so bad that God will not forgive you." Reid was ecstatic, he knew these things but seemed to have forgotten them because he was distracted, trying to do his own thing.

Christmas break was approaching and Reid decided to return home as a surprise. Sunday morning service had begun and his dad was up ministering the word. Reid walked through the door and his dad stopped preaching; he stepped down from the pulpit and gave his son the biggest hug. Reid whispered in his dad's ear, "Father I have sinned against heaven and you. I am no longer worthy to be called your son." His mom was in tears and began thanking God like never before. The church began to rejoice because they knew they were looking at the work of the Lord.

Reid told his parents the story of how he felt growing up

until that day. He felt as if he could not do anything as a child. They explained to him that there were certain things they allowed and some they didn't (But like my daughter, he had only seen what he couldn't do). He told his parents that once he joined this new religion, he always felt a void, like he was empty. His mom explained the reason why. She said it was because Jesus is the only one who can fill that void. Reid's parents had laid the foundation for their son. He went astray like we all have at one time or another in our Christian walk. But with God being sovereign He allowed the Holy Spirit to prick Reid's heart and draw him back to the cross What an amazing God we serve.

Jane

Jane, having grown up in a small, country town, was determined to leave once she graduated high school. She had dreams of going to college and becoming a nurse. Jane was not your typical teenager, after school she would go volunteer at the local nursing home where she assisted in caring for the elderly. Her parents, Herbert and June, had always taught her to treat others with the utmost respect. Unfortunately, on the approach of graduation, her parents were in a horrific accident, leaving only Herbert alive, albeit paralyzed from the neck down. Overwhelmed with choosing between remaining at home as her father's full-time caregiver or pursuing her dream to be a nurse, Jane did the only thing she knew to be certain. She prayed. Undoubtedly, Jane heard from her Lord, saying, "My daughter, take care of your father as I will take care of you," and she knew in her heart that she had no choice. One day at a time, she cared for her father, she attended class, and she hired nurses to tend to her dad while she was away from the house in class. Remembering the prayer she prayed years before, Jane persevered through the mounting responsibilities.

Ultimately, Jane's sacrifice, determination, and heart of love led her to open her own senior care center named for her mom *For The Love of June Assisted Living Center*.

Although our plan may be aligned with God's plan, He may allow us to take a different pathway to fulfill it.

Mike

Mike, a U.S. Marine, had finished his training and was stationed overseas. The nightlife was real to him. He would complete his job at the end of the week and then the drinking, clubbing, and womanizing would begin. Mike would get so wasted he could not recall anything, and unfortunately, it soon began to affect his work performance. Self-professed "too much man for just one woman", Mike had always bragged that he would never settle down with one woman.

With his excessive drinking taking a toll on him, he began showing up late for formation. Soon, Mike was demoted, assigned additional duties, and saw a decrease in his pay. One day while Mike was on extra duty, Sergeant Jacobs pulled him to the side and asked him what he was doing with his life. Always a hot-head, Mike blurted out a trail of excuses, but Sergeant Jacobs told him he needed to think about what he was doing to his life.

Four years later, Mike's time had ended in the military. Having had enough of military life, he chose not to re-enlist. One day Mike remembered the advice that Sergeant Jacobs gave him regarding the direction of his life. Although time had passed, Mike had remained friends with some of the guys in the Marines, one in particular named Todd, had invited him to church. Mike attended and enjoyed it, so he continued to go Sunday after Sunday. Noticing the choir director, Mike inquired about her, her name was Cindy. Todd, who was married, told him she was single, and Mike's interest in Cindy soon grew each week.

One Sunday after church, Mike walked up to her and introduced himself, but she didn't seem interested. Mike didn't like that because he was accustomed to women returning his attraction. Obviously, that life was over. Sundays passed and he continued to speak to Cindy and compliment her on how nice of a job she was doing at directing the choir. One day he asked her out for Sunday dinner. She accepted. Mike and Cindy started to spend more and more time together, quickly realizing that they had so much in common. Mike proposed marriage and she willingly accepted. They got married and had three beautiful girls.

Back when Mike was in the military, he said he would never settle down, but once we allow the Holy Spirit to work in us and change us, God will show up and show out.

William

William was drafted into the NFL at the age of eighteen. He thought the sky was the limit, but God had other plans. William enjoyed traveling with the team and the bonds that they formed over the course of the season. Furthermore, as the quarterback, he was setting records with pass attempts, pass completions, and passing yards. He sat at the top of his career by the age of 25.

During his final game of the season, William hiked the ball, dropped back to ready himself for the pass, and found himself staring at the oversized lights above. He had been sacked. As he lay on the wet field, his whole career flashed before his eyes. Finding it difficult to breathe and move, William had no idea about the extent of his injuries. Soon, the coaches and other players rushed onto the field, but at only a quick glance, Coach Davenport knew William needed more help than they could give. Having signaled for the emergency response team and watching as they carefully lifted him onto the stretcher, Coach Davenport, the team, and fans gazed at the exiting ambulance in shock. Coach Gaines, the assistant coach, rode with William in the ambulance, he listened as William yelled at the top of his lungs in pain. X-rays showed his left rib broken in what doctors called one of the most serious cases they had ever seen.

Once the news of his injury and the unlikelihood of continuing in his career were explained, he sat devastated. Days crept by as William began healing and working on his strength during physical therapy. Depressed about his new situation, William soon began to wallow in his circumstances, claiming football to be all he knew, thus leaving him with no reason to live. Although his coaches and friends would visit him, their time there didn't seem to cheer him up. One night William was lying in his bed and his mind ran back to times that they would have prayer before each game. William opened his mouth and began to speak. "I don't want to live anymore, but I know if I kill myself, people will miss me. If there is a God up there, give me a sign of why I should live." After that prayer, Nurse Leila walked in his room and told him her son, Justin was a huge fan of his and asked him if she could get his autograph. He signed the autograph, and once she left he looked up, asking, "Is that the sign?" The next day Leila came by and asked if she could bring Justin to meet him, and William agreed.

The next morning, William heard a light knock on the door, and he said, "Come in." It was Leila and Justin. He was so excited to meet William that he asked him all types of questions. At the end of the visit, Justin asked if William could come speak to his school for Career Day once he was released from the hospital. William did not turn down the invitation. He really enjoyed the visit. The next month William was released from the hospital, and as he exited, he gave Leila his telephone number so that Justin's school could call him for Career Day. The school soon called William to schedule the assembly. William went to the school and spoke, he also allowed time for Q&A.

From that day on, William began receiving calls from different people wanting to book him for speaking engagements. William became a motivational speaker, telling others not to give up on life simply because they hit a bump in the road or because something didn't turn out the way they thought it should have.

Carmen

Carmen knew that once she was done with Catholic School, she would move to New York and go to school for dance. She had to get away. She had had enough of the "God thing." She had pictures hanging up in her room of famous dancers, and that was what she always dreamed of being ever since she could remember. She could recall in chapel every Friday, hearing a still small voice say, "I want you in full-time ministry. I want you to become a nun." She would blow it off and pretend not to hear it. God was tugging on her.

Carmen applied to school without her parents knowing, but she was rejected. She really wanted to go to that particular one, so she applied again and was rejected again. Carmen continued to run from her calling until one day at school, at the end of the year—Career Day. The nuns were asking everyone what they planned on doing once they graduated. It was Carmen's turn.

She said with a whisper, "I'm going to become a nun." Everyone turned around and looked at her, the teacher asked her to say it a little louder because she did not hear her. As Carmen bit down on her nails, she spoke more clearly this time and repeated, "I'm going to become a nun." With eyes open wide and mouths dropped, the nuns began to applaud. Carmen wondered why such a big commotion for her. After class ended Sister Mary Joseph came up to her and shared, "I am so happy that you accepted your calling." Carmen began to weep, covering her face as tears filled her hands. Sister Mary Joseph embraced her. Carmen asked her what were her next steps.

While Carmen had one plan, God had another. He saw something in her that she did not see in herself, and that was to be used as a vessel by Him.

Stefan

Stefan grew up in a single parent home where he was told that he would never do anything with his life, that he would be a low life like his dad. Unfortunately, Stefan bought into those negative declarations by joining a gang, which encouraged him to rob, stab, and even kill others, all in an effort to establish himself as a leader in the organization. Stefan had become very angry with the people he grew up around, and he cut no one any slack. If he saw someone stepping out of line, he would direct others to inflict harm in one way or another, never allowing that someone to fight back.

One day a rival gang decided to come after Stefan and his members because they heard Stefan and a few other gang members had been disrespecting them; it turned out to be a really gruesome scene with five lives lost. Stefan was arrested as a suspect, and the judge found him guilty. Stefan spent seven years in prison where he began to take anger management classes and he also came to terms with the issues in his childhood. He even used that time to further develop himself and his education through college courses, an art class and worship service. While incarcerated, Stefan never had any contact with the outside world because no one ever came to visit him.

As part of Stefan's punishment, in addition to being in jail, he had to mentor youth at a local recreation center. Stefan spoke to the young men and told them they did not want to follow the path he had chosen. One day at the recreation center, they had Art Day and all were encouraged to bring in anything they had created as a work of art. Stefan took in one of the pieces that he had painted. He had no idea there would be buyers from the local museum there. When the buyers approached Stefan's piece of art, they didn't know who it belonged to. Stefan stood up and claimed it.

Soon, Stefan had paid his debt to society and was released from incarceration. Once he was released, Mr. Stanley from the event contacted Stefan and informed him that they wanted him to become a painter for them. He assumed the company was hiring him to paint buildings, but he was wrong. Mr. Stanley and his associates said, "No, you do great work, and we have buyers from all over the country who contact us about specific pieces they are looking for.

We have to search for those pieces for them, but if we had you on staff, you could just paint them right then."

Stefan could not believe that the graffiti work he was doing as a gang member would pay off like this. The men did not care about his past; they were concerned about his future. Stefan immediately thanked the men, and once he was alone, he said a prayer. "Lord, thank you for giving me another chance." No matter what you've been through, God can still use you.

Claire

Claire had been working for the company 25 years. Although she had heard rumors of the company laying off, she paid no attention to it. One morning Claire arrived at work like she normally did. She sat at her desk and opened her e-mail to find a message regarding her being laid off. Claire was distraught, and she felt betrayed because she believed she had given this company so much of her life. The email went on to say that she would receive pay for her vacation as well as a severance package. Claire could not believe this was happening to her. The email also read that she would be released from her duties in two weeks.

The end of the two weeks soon arrived, and Claire felt like her life had stopped. She pictured herself on the edge of a cliff, not knowing whether to walk left, which would be to move back home, or walk right, which would be to stay still and listen for directions from God. She decided to walk right and be still. As each day passed Claire awakened each morning like clockwork and did her devotions. One morning she woke up and decided she would go to her local children's hospital and start to volunteer. This was something new for Claire; she had never worked with children.

The hospital placed her with terminally ill children who were confined to wheelchairs. She would play games and read stories to them. Claire inquired about why the children weren't getting out doing things outside instead of always being cooped up in the hospital. The staff explained to her that allowing the patients to play outside would put the hospital and the children at risk of increased sickness or danger. So Claire went home that night and brainstormed. She wondered what she could do or what business she could start that would give back to the kids. Claire finally decided on an indoor pool where the children would still be in the building but would be given the opportunity to feel as if they were outside.

Claire began to write out the business plan. She had to determine several factors, including how the project would be funded, the number and qualifications of lifeguards on duty, and the training for the nurses that would be assisting the children in the pool. This would also be therapy for them. Claire completed the plan and presented it to the hospital board. They told her that it was a great idea. The pool was built and they brought Claire on staff as the director over the pool.

　　Claire only knew her previous job as her life. Once she lost it she felt that her life was over. She was confused and did not know which way to go. She stood fast and waited for direction from God and he came through for her.

Brian

Brian, an attorney by day and a male dancer by night, lived what many would call a double life. Although he had been practicing law for nearly 12 years, no one knew of his other life. It started out as needing extra money to pay for law school and then he just continued. He felt addicted to it. He loved the attention he received while dancing, the women throwing money at him all the time. After the night ended, he would go back to his inanimate house and do it all over again; practice law during the day and dance at night.

One night he went to work and noticed a bachelorette party going on in the lounge. They requested him as a dancer; he walked over and started his show. He noticed that one of the women was Miriam, a Judge he had stood before the previous week and presented a case to in court. He was in total shock but did not stop the show. Once he was finished, he hurried out quickly, but she ran after him and asked him why he was working there. After explaining why he was dancing, Miriam had a very disappointed look on her face. He also told her he wanted to stop but felt addicted to it and couldn't.

The next day, he had to go before her again in court. Once court was adjourned, she asked if she could speak with him in her chambers. Miriam told him she had been praying for him and wanted to invite him to church. He told her no, that someone like him would not be accepted in church. The next time she saw him in court, she invited him again, and this time he accepted. She gave him the address, and they met there.

As Brian walked in church he felt as if everyone was looking at him. The guilt of living a double life was getting to him. Miriam noticed that he was uncomfortable, and assured him that no one was looking at him. As the service continued he became more relaxed. Towards the end of service he leaned over to let her know that he enjoyed the message. At this time Pastor Reilly opened the doors of the church and called for anyone who would like to know Jesus as their personal Savior to come forward. The pastor reminded them that they had not done anything so bad that God could not forgive them. Immediately, he began to feel the tears in his eyes roll down his face. He went to the altar that day and accepted Christ into his life. Soon, he quit the job as a dancer because he felt convicted.

Years passed as he went around evangelizing to others of how God changed his life. Brian went back to his job at the club and invited his old coworkers to church; he was so excited he wanted to tell everyone.

Brian was getting more involved in church, taking leadership classes and working alongside Pastor Reilly. Brian's new life in Christ was even affecting the way he handled cases in court. It was no longer about the money and how many cases he could take in, it was about sharing the word of God and letting them know their lives could be different. They didn't have to continue down the same path of unrighteousness. One Sunday morning he went in to speak with the pastor before service, and told him he was going to accept his calling as a pastor. He felt such a heavy weight had been lifted from him, because he still remembered his past. He realized that day he accepted Christ that he was dirty/unclean, but he was not too dirty for God to clean him up.

As you can see from these stories, you don't have to be perfect to accept Jesus Christ as your personal Savior. You simply need to be willing, open and ready for change.

First John 1:9 states, if we confess our sins; he is faithful and just to forgive us our sins, and to cleanse us from all unrighteousness. Accept him into your heart today and let him change your life forever.

Daily Walk: Colossians 2:6-7 So then, just as you received Christ Jesus as Lord, continue to live your lives in him, rooted and built up in him, strengthened in the faith as you were taught, and overflowing with thankfulness.

Faith: 1 Corinthians 16:13-14 Be on your guard; stand firm in the faith; be courageous; be strong. Do everything in love.

Grace: Ephesians 2:8 For it is by grace you have been saved, through faith – and this is not from yourselves, it is the gift of God – not of works, so that no one can boast.

Love: Psalm 103:17 But from everlasting to everlasting the LORD's love is with those who fear him, and his righteousness with their children's children.

Future writings: Promises From God

Stay connected with Sepsimone

Contact info: sepsimonejohnson.webs.com
www.facebook.com/sepsimonejohnson
sepsimonejohnson@gmail.com

Renewed For Purpose Ministries
P.O. Box 382685
Duncanville, TX 75138

Made in the USA
Lexington, KY
03 June 2014